CONTENTS

D0274168

THE DEEP OCEAN

Very little is known about the deepest parts of the ocean and the animals that live there. In fact, there is no other place on the planet that we know so little about.

The deepest part of the ocean is the Mariana Trench. It is about 11,000 metres deep. Mount Everest is the highest mountain in the world. If Mount Everest was placed inside the Mariana Trench, it would not reach the surface of the ocean.

Sometimes unusual deep-sea creatures wash up onto beaches. They get caught in fishing nets, too. These strange animals make people wonder about what lives at the bottom of the ocean. Scientists exploring the ocean continue to discover sea life that has never been seen before by people.

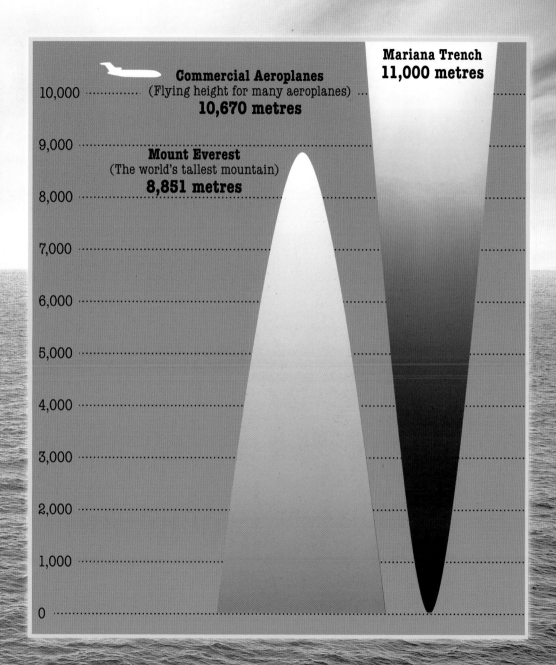

Commercial Aeroplanes
(Flying height for many aeroplanes)
10,670 metres

Mariana Trench
11,000 metres

Mount Everest
(The world's tallest mountain)
8,851 metres

10,000

9,000

8,000

7,000

6,000

5,000

4,000

3,000

2,000

1,000

0

DEEP-SEA EXPLORATION

In recent years, scientists have built small vehicles that can go underwater. These are called *submersibles*. Some submersibles do not carry passengers. Because there is no one on board, they are run by *remote control*. They use special cameras to film creatures that swim by. Some submersibles even have remote-control arms that can pick up things that they find.

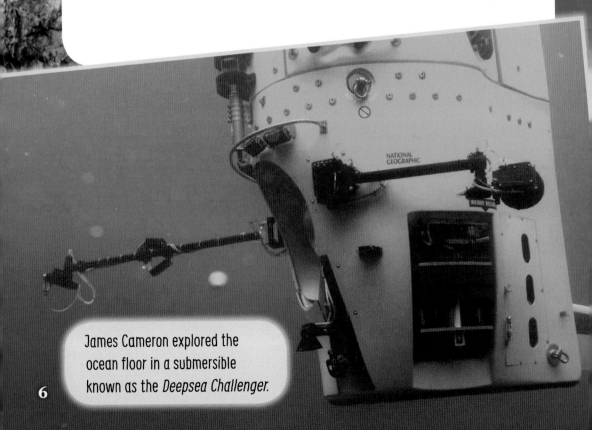

James Cameron explored the ocean floor in a submersible known as the *Deepsea Challenger*.

In March 2012, film director James Cameron became the first person to travel in a submersible to the bottom of the Mariana Trench. He went down almost 11 kilometres from the surface of the ocean.

Cameron was the first person to spend several hours exploring the depths of the Mariana Trench. He was able to collect rocks and small sea creatures. This has helped scientists study deep-sea creatures in their natural *habitats* or surroundings.

FACT James Cameron has won many awards for the films he's written and directed. His films include *Titanic*, *The Terminator*, and *Avatar*.

James Cameron

Edith Widder is a famous *oceanographer*. She is a scientist who studies the ocean and the plants and animals that live there.

She uses coloured lights to attract unusual deep-sea creatures. The lights flash inside a ball that is made to look like a jellyfish. Widder calls the ball the E-jelly. In the darkness of the deep ocean, sea creatures are attracted to the colourful lights.

Widder and her team of scientists wait in their submersible while creatures from the deep come to them. They have studied, filmed, and taken photos of some amazing sea creatures.

In 2012, Edith Widder and her team filmed a giant squid off the coast of Japan. This was the first time a giant squid had ever been caught on film in its natural habitat. They used the E-jelly to attract the squid while they filmed it from a submersible nearby.

Oceanographer Edith Widder examines a camera that is used to explore the bottom of the ocean.

THE DEEP-SEA ENVIRONMENT

Researchers are faced with many problems when they explore the deepest parts of the ocean. First, the water temperature is near freezing. It is also so far beneath the ocean's surface that there is no sunlight at all. It is very dark, and there is very little *oxygen*, which we need to breathe.

bigeye houndshark

There is also a lot of *pressure* at the bottom of the ocean. Pressure is like a huge weight that crushes things in very deep water.

Many sea creatures that we see in shallow water avoid the deepest parts of the ocean because of the pressure. Animals that live at the bottom of the ocean have bodies that can handle the pressure. However, most of them cannot survive if they are brought up to the surface. Their bodies need the pressure of the deep water in order to work properly.

blot

WEIRD AND WONDERFUL CREATURES

Some animals that live in the deepest parts of the ocean can do amazing things. For example, some creatures can make their own light. They use this light to attract prey in the darkness. Animals that come close to the light get eaten!

deep-sea jellyfish

helmet jellyfish

The stoplight loosejaw

The stoplight loosejaw is a very unusual deep-sea creature that makes its own light. It is a small fish that has two patches under its eyes that make red light.

Most creatures that live in the deepest parts of the ocean cannot see red light. The stoplight loosejaw uses its red light to see prey in the darkness. Because the prey cannot see the red light, it doesn't even know that it's being watched.

The stoplight loosejaw has a very large mouth. When it opens its mouth, it shoots out its bottom jaw and swallows its prey.

stoplight loosejaw

The anglerfish

The anglerfish is another interesting creature found in the deepest parts of the world's oceans. The word "angler" means someone who goes fishing with a fishing rod. If you look closely at the anglerfish, you can see how it got this name.

A deep-sea anglerfish prepares to capture its prey.

The female anglerfish is usually dark grey or brown in colour. It has a long horn or spike growing out of the top of its mouth. On the end of this spike, there is a little piece of skin that the anglerfish can wiggle. The skin gives off light in the dark sea that other fish swim towards.

The anglerfish wiggles this tiny bit of skin. Then it waits for a hungry fish to come along and try to eat the wiggling skin. When the fish gets close, the anglerfish opens its huge mouth and swallows the prey whole. Some anglerfish can open their jaws so wide that they can eat fish that are twice their size.

an angler

There are more than 200 different types of anglerfish. Most are less than 30 centimetres long, but some grow to more than 90 centimetres long. Many of them live in cold, dark water near the bottom of the ocean. But some live in warm water much closer to the surface.

FACT Male anglerfish are very different from the females. They are very small and do not catch other fish. Instead, the males attach themselves to one of the females. They feed on the female's blood.

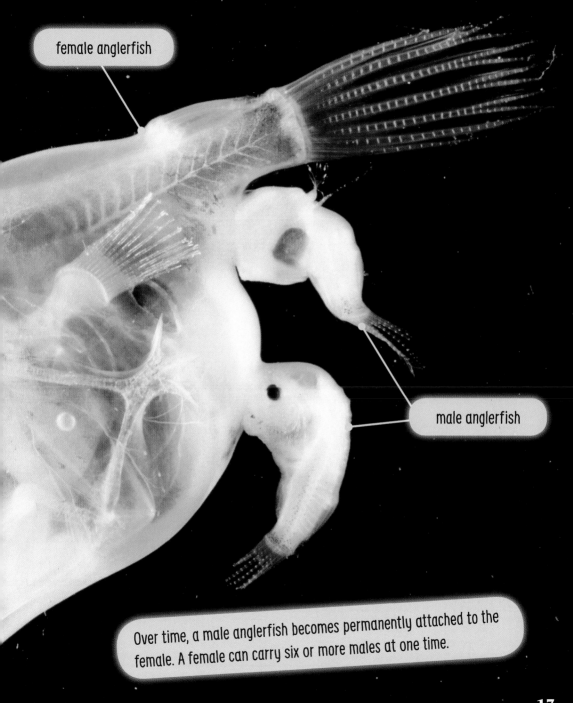

female anglerfish

male anglerfish

Over time, a male anglerfish becomes permanently attached to the female. A female can carry six or more males at one time.

The giant isopod

Giant isopods are found in the deep, dark water at the bottom of oceans. They look a lot like woodlice but can grow up to 40 centimetres long.

a giant isopod

woodlouse

A giant isopod curls up into a ball for protection.

Giant isopods have hard outer shells made of several pieces. They curl up into a ball and crawl inside their shells to stay safe from prey.

Giant isopods have two *antennae* or feelers on their heads. They use these to find food. Giant isopods eat meat. They are also *scavengers*. This means they eat the remains of dead creatures.

Giant isopods can eat a large amount when food is easy to find. They can also go for a long time without eating. A giant isopod in Japan once went five years without eating a single thing!

Female giant isopods lay eggs. They carry the eggs in a small pouch on their undersides. The young stay in this pouch until they are big enough to care for themselves. When they leave the pouch, they look just like adult isopods only much smaller.

Giant isopods are part of the same animal family as shrimps and crabs.

The pelican eel

In 2003, scientists studied creatures living in the deep waters between Australia and New Zealand. One of the animals they found was the pelican eel.

The pelican eel has a huge mouth filled with rows of very tiny teeth. Like the anglerfish, the pelican eel can open its mouth very wide. The pelican eel uses its mouth like a net to catch its prey.

The pelican eel eats shrimp, small fish, and squid. Its stomach can hold a lot of food.

The pelican eel is black and has a very long tail. It can grow to be about 60 centimetres long. The pelican eel has tiny eyes, so it cannot see very well. It uses its sense of smell to find food.

Through its skin, the pelican eel is able to feel the movement of other creatures in the water. A small red tip at the end of the pelican eel's tail lights up. Like the anglerfish, the pelican eel uses this light to attract prey.

The giant squid

Giant squid are huge creatures that live in very deep water. For hundreds of years, fishermen have told stories about sea monsters large enough to drag ships underwater. These sea monsters were most likely giant squid.

Giant squid have been found in many parts of the world. However, they do not live in very warm seas or close to the North and South Poles.

Giant squid are hardly ever seen alive. Sometimes the body of a dead giant squid will wash up onto a beach or get caught in a fishing net. This gives scientists the chance to learn about these huge creatures.

The largest giant squid that scientists have measured was more than 12 metres long and weighed nearly 900 kilograms.

Researchers used a fake squid (lower right) to attract a 7-metre-long giant squid about 965 kilometres off the coast of Japan.

Giant squid have eight arms and two longer feeding *tentacles*. The squid can shoot out its armlike tentacles a long distance to grab prey. The tentacles are covered with suckers. Each sucker has a ring of tiny hooks that are shaped like pointy teeth. This makes it very difficult for prey to wiggle free once caught in a giant squid's tentacles.

The giant squid's tentacles have sharp, pointy suckers.

The giant squid has very large eyes that can be as big as a basketball! These eyes help the giant squid to see prey in the darkness.

a giant squid's eye

The giant squid's mouth looks like a bird's beak. Inside is a tongue, or *radula*, that is covered in rows of sharp teeth. The giant squid pulls the prey towards its mouth, and then eats it with the toothy tongue. Giant squid eat fish, other squid and shrimp.

a giant squid's mouth or beak

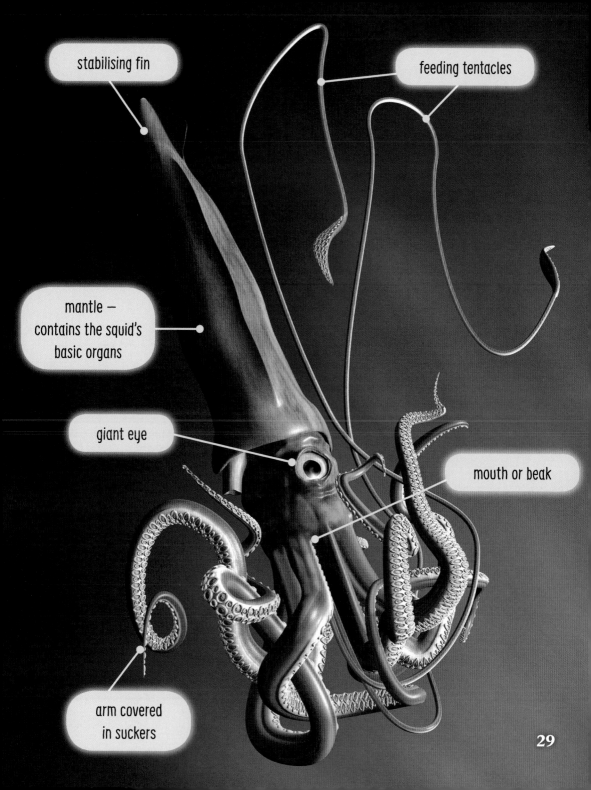

stabilising fin

feeding tentacles

mantle —
contains the squid's
basic organs

giant eye

mouth or beak

arm covered
in suckers

29

MORE TO DISCOVER

Much research is being carried out, but we still know very little about the deepest parts of the ocean. However, we do know that there is a lot more life at the bottom of the sea than people ever imagined. We can also be fairly sure that there are many creatures that are still waiting to be discovered!

An oceanographer does research in a deep-sea submersible.

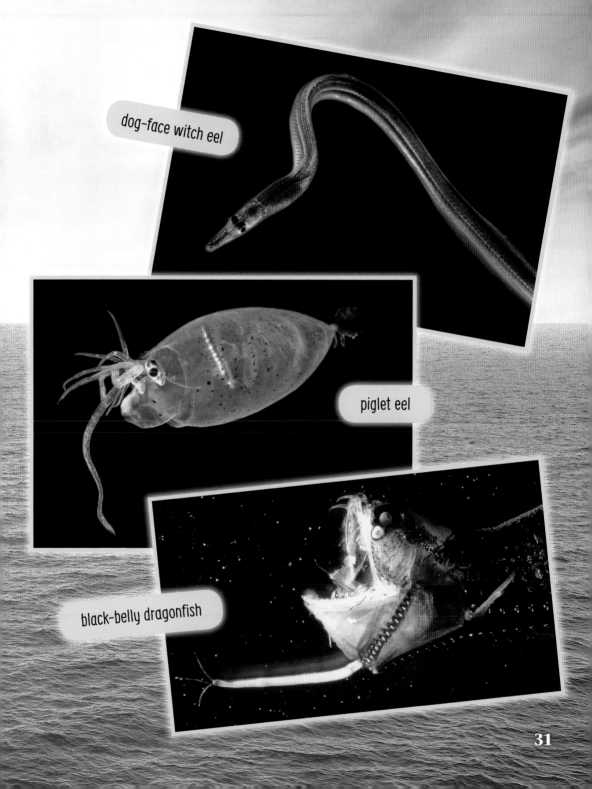

dog-face witch eel

piglet eel

black-belly dragonfish

GLOSSARY

antenna feeler on a sea creature's head that is used to sense movement

habitat natural place and conditions in which a plant or animal lives

oceanographer scientist who studies the ocean and ocean life

oxygen colourless gas that people and animals need to breathe

pressure force produced by pressing on something

radula tongue covered in sharp teeth

remote control device used to control machines from a distance

scavenger animal that eats dead things

submersible small vessel used underwater, usually for research

tentacle long, armlike body part that some animals use to touch, grab, or smell

INDEX